Invocations and Other Love Songs

Christine Berger

Letters

Concrescent Letters

Invocations and Other Love Songs © 2014 Chrstine Berger

For information contact:
Concrescent Letters, an imprint of Concrescent LLC
Richmond CA, USA
info@Concrescent.net

ISBN: 978-0-9903927-0-5

Library of Congress Control Number: 2014940164

Opening Prayer to Hermes
04-07-12

As I open,
Will You open the way before me?
As You open the way before me,
Will You open me as well?

As I open,
Will You open the way before me?
As You open the way before me,
Will You open me as well?

As I open,
Will You open the way before me?
As You open the way before me,
Will You open me as well?

As I open,
Will You open the way before me?
As You open the way before me,
Will You open me as well?

  This collection of poems is a result of Hermes
stepping into my life in bright living color April of
2012. Groundwork for that had been laid in February at
Pantheacon where many of us gathered to talk about
serving the community as His priests and priestesses.
My life changed. The opening prayer to Hermes was the
first encounter, and given to me by Him when I was
on lunch break driving near work. There were following
occasions where He came to me with more energy than
I had imagined and I stood hyperventilating over my
kitchen sink. This was just the beginning.

In the summer came a time when I met a Priestess
of His and many of the Greek Gods and Goddesses as
well as Loki online through the Hermes Group. Quite
rapidly I was drawn into fulfilling a promise I had made
to her lifetimes ago to come to her aid when she was

in crisis. Though unprepared I invoked my Higher Self and any aspect within known or unknown to serve that purpose. These poems written in 2012 are a result of that time of a magical war. There has never been any time in any lifetime to compare to that period. It took a long time to recover from and process. This book is born of that time when I was changed in the name of Love that would withhold nothing.

Many of the invocations and poems are channeled. Some from my Higher Self who was in the driver's seat constantly and some by the Deities, and other Beings. I asked for clearance from all involved before bringing this book out.

May this writing and any writing that I bring to public eye be of benefit to all.

Hermes

invocation to Hermes

God wounded-God Healed

Immersion

Interceding Messenger

of Gods and Men

The Herm Stood

Who am I Speaking For?

Invocation
04-07-12

Heart Awakening
Love Instigator
Holder of the Boundaries
Transcender of the Boundaries
Matrix Supporter
Quantum Spinner
Field Unifier
Rider of the Winds
Transmitter of thought and word
You whose target practice is perfect
You whose target is both center and universal
You who enlivens
You who navigates
You who course corrects
You who trail blazes
Bringer of Joy
Bringer of ecstasy
Bringer of peace
Bringer of the still mind
Bringer of the mind lit by lightning flashes
Comforter
Rabble-rouser
Guide and Teacher

Thank you for holding the journey
for my heart to travel this day.

God-wounded, God-healed
10-31-12

I was driving down the road
Thinking about my life
Thinking about this unquenchable fire at the heart of it
Thinking and feeling into the center of it
How the passion burns and the longing consumes
God-wounded is what I am
Then I heard you say
God-wounded, God-healed

The summer stripped me down
Revealed my purpose
Exposed my gifts and my love under fire
Showed me that Gods and men
are under the skin the same
Though you are beings with super powers
You love you grieve you triumph you learn
When I grow up I want to be just like you
Except in a me shape
God-wounded, God-healed

I have seen the sacred fire
bring warmth and healing
I have seen it destroy with impunity
and equal fervor
I have felt the strength of compassion
and the terror of grief that is akin to madness
because its intensity cannot be relieved
I have witnessed more than I was able to perceive
Without being turned inside out for the better
God-wounded, God-healed

I have seen the lightning's flashing
Felt it tear through me to free my Spirit
Left me trembling without power for a day
But safe and sheltered as careless as a child
I have tasted freedom as if a bird in flight
Sheltered in the arms of a lover
As limitless as the night
Tasted ambrosia for a moment
and had utter respite from even the thought of duality
God-wounded, God-healed

Immersion
03-19-13

For hours immersing myself
in all these words
As if buried somewhere within them
There were some truth about Gods and men
That could be of value for the next traveler
In reality I will never know if those who read them
Find a glimmer of themselves
or a taste of something sweet and fierce
To help them stay warm on a deep cold night

What I seek to convey
Is a song as fine as a soft warm blanket
Created from the Love conveyed in those quiet spaces
The ones that you fall into in the middle of deep meditation
Only to be thrust back into consciousness
By that Aspect which had pushed you aside that it
could leave its imprint
Without interference or explanation

If I learned nothing else last year
in the summer of my passion and transformation
Through the pure grace of the Gods
Is that we are not different in nature
But only in degree of the amount of energy we can manifest
in this world
and the impact that it has

We Love
We Create
We Grieve
We Regret
We Recreate ourselves to be the finest clearest visioned
pure-hearted
Beings that we can be
The merging that gives us Joy
Gives the Gods Joy
The communication that feeds us
Feeds Them
That which we feel
They feel as well
And we feel more of Them than we are conscious of

For me this year is a year of brick and mortar
Of work on self, and shaping
Of sifting through the rubbish and finding the jewels
I do my best to be slow and thoughtful and to take care
So that the end result will show the beauty and
strength of the journey

Interceding Messenger
11-09-12

Like a forest fire this desire
Blazes through the corridors of body and mind
laying waste to all impediments
to our union
My imagination is taken
as if on a long journey
all is aglow under the influence of a golden sun
the walls and floors designed as a temple
pillars and columns of massive design
Where is this place that my soul seeks?

There is a sensation of souring
of taking flight
of being lifted
all my senses fully engaged
This is not a leave taking of the body
But an elevation of the body itself
Perhaps a fire is lit under it and within it
and it rises in the way that a hot air balloon would rise
Full and buoyant and light as air

Who has come to me in the midst of my work day?
Who has carved me a niche in which to taste such freedom?
Who holds me so tenderly in the hand of Love
The bond is One upon One
I have tasted this vibration this flavor
Once before
In a time between the worlds
and it is good
It has healing and revelation and transformation
as its innermost structure
It cannot be anything other than these
It is its very nature

This is how it happens
This is Love in Action in Motion in Secret Places
I can allude to that which Is
But I am merely narrating a story to correspond
To these ecstatic currents which have swept me away

This taste of ambrosia will surely feed my soul
as a great banquet with the finest companions
would feed my human spirit
with joy and comfort and peace.

Thank you Oh Joyous One!!

Of Gods and Men
08-30-12

An hour and a half conversation
as well as transmission of my Patron Hermes
To a new (to me) aspect of Dorothea
Brought healing and revelation and understanding

So although the grief more brought by shock
Than loss
(even though both are at play)
has not disappeared
I am calmer
Though so much in the future is uncertain
I know Who I belong to
and with the conscious acknowledgment of my Higher Self
I pray that I can know who I am and live from the
space of the Heart
more fully
Each and every day

As witness to so much
revolution and evolution in the life of my heart sister
and the Gods we both adore and serve
I have seen wheels within wheels
Each day a new secret exposed
A nuance that was before overlooked
An important soul piece found and plans for rescue
From the root cause of the madness

There is a glimmer of understanding unfolding
Though my Higher Self may have firm grasp on it
I am understanding in bits and pieces
The magnificence of this Universe
and that Gods need conscious humans
Just as humans will die without conscious contact
and service to the Gods

It is this reawakening on both our parts
Gods and men
That gives me hope

I can taste the energy of cohesion between us
and the joy and sweetness of knowing how very very much
We love each other and
need each other's viewpoint
I never understood before that the Big Picture and
vantage point
of the Gods
Needs have balance from those of us living caught in
time and space
On the earth
It teases at my consciousness in this moment
And the revelation of it more fully will bring the ecstasy
of the mind
When connections burst to the surface

Meanwhile may every God and Goddess
Who has loved me
this lifetime and others
Who has reached out to me when it was so dark
so bleak and so difficult for me
this lifetime and others
Know all the energy and love and devotion and respect
That I carry
As a blessing for Them
Wherever They may be

Without You I would not breathe
I would not dance
I would not know the true power of Love
I would not have been supported until
My Higher Self and I could connect
Would not have tasted the union of us
In the deepest heart of the silence

May neither You nor I ever forget this Love between us
It is the glue that holds all together

The Herm Stood
02-27-13

The Herm stood
where it stood was the crossroads
the center of the Universe
Just as Yggdrasil
stands
Born in the mind of the First God
All worlds became manifest
at that First Word

It waited, this Herm, essential
within the cellular structure of the finest Douglas fir
it waited for the tree to grow
for the Priesthood to be ready
for the Priest ready to say YES
It is time to have this manifest
This the presence of the God
brought forth in the community of Men
To mark the crossroads between the worlds
to shatter the illusion that these days
cannot hold the current as well as those ancient days
When men and Gods were the closest of family

Service blending with darshan
Inspiration with open hearts and minds and the will
To keep the practice of the God arising
at the heart of daily life
the cycles of the year
Each having a place to make sacrifice
and to honor the wellspring of life
the One
manifest as the All

There was joy in the carving
in the raising up
in the occupation
as the God came down
as this symbolic merging of form
and Divine energy
became real
and activated by all the Love of those who came
To say thank you
To petition
To celebrate
to chat, with this Power we call the Friendly God

Tonight within meditation
I felt the Herm call
Invoking the God
I felt the Herm vibrating
Its life a cohesive force in the neighborhood
May these words convey a bit of all that was felt in
that moment.
May the work we as individuals in community practice
Bring the change
and humans and Gods walk together again

For all who have eyes to see and partake in
the sacred life.

For all who may benefit.

Who Am I Speaking For?
11-03-12

If I am fully engaged in the silence
Which holds and heals and keeps alignment
Then words will be few and flow from guidance
In that space I can learn as ebb and flow do their dance
And the light of my companions is the light at the
center of my being

To some degree it is always a struggle for me
To be in a large group of people
Especially in these days of foundation and reconstruction
I have forgotten how to keep my energy from flowing outward
While holding firmly to the energies within at heart and
womb at feet and crown
When I get off track I forget myself
and the words that escape from my mouth do not serve
my intent

This being said, if I am to be lost in moments
Those that I love are the ones who allow me the feeling
of safety
as bits and fragments of shadow escape as I navigate
inner and outer
Worlds in whatever mix is presenting
Part of my work at this time is to be gentle with myself
and stay chilled and undemanding of any particular result
As I do this paint by numbers redesigning

How do I proceed?
I listen
There are clues everywhere
I have not left this world and then returned
I burrowed deeper into it and tasted and drank and was nourished
Most of my struggle these days is only because I was thrust
to the surface too quickly and traumatically at the end
So like the deep sea diver I suffer from the bends

As it gets better little by little
Firmly embracing the structure which has grown
Over the years in practices to ground me in Spirit and Love
It is important and indeed critical
That I spend time with the finest friends I could
possibly have
and listen and know there is no difference in our struggles
Each is re-birthing themselves with the influx of energy
that increases daily

I was told this last night but was not able to pass it on
to the person I had in my heart at the time
"Simplify your activity, cut down to the core necessities,
Something new is opening for you,
Just make the space in yourself and in your life
and let it arrive in its own time"

Dionysus

Dionysus
08-17-12

Dangerous and beautiful
Just a glance in Your direction
and I am captured
Unable to define that which overcomes me
My secrets revealed
My desires at the forefront
Emotions running rampant
You smile, then laugh
Reminding me once again that what You do best
Is reveal myself to me

Lord of the vineyards
You Yourself a conduit to ecstasy
Have not neglected me because the path of drugs and wine
Is no longer open to me
I have not forgotten the nights of almost death
The great revelations that body and soul paid for
The fearlessness and determination that I carried
In that youthful Heart
To know You

Still You thrill
with no effort at all my pulse races
my breath quickens
So easy to detect Your presence
Though not the easiest God to receive
Much like a village in the path of the Tsunami
I find myself both aroused and terrified
With no place to run
Yet there is that within me that does not fear you

Those who call You mad do not know
You are the essence of raw emotion
When You grieve, You grieve fully
When You are angry, You rage
Your justice is fierce, relentless and utterly complete
There is no separation between the passion you carry
and the Passion You are

We mortals who are half alive
are drawn to You that we may truly taste what Life is
Knowing what Life is,
Leading us to the edge between Life and Death
You would teach us to be poised there
as long as mortal flesh and mind can bear
Because it is on that razor's edge that Spirit can break free
and though we must shield our eyes
The Light of it blazes through us
and we recognize and embrace
The reverberations of Your haunting revelation at last

Oh Dionysus
08-20-12

Since last night I am not certain you have ever left my thoughts
At work sitting here and questioning
Whether there was any love in my last love affair
I realized that there is still a great deal I have neither uncovered
Nor let go of yet
and in stating my willingness to do so
I thought about a statement I read yesterday
That we attract wounded lovers as long as we are
wounded ourselves

A flash through my mind
That you, sweet Dionysus
By showing us the weight you carry
Are the best example there is of courage
in the face of emotions that we think we cannot bear
Perhaps that was what you were trying to show me last night
Though some of the expression of your pain
Was too horrific for me to see

No, I am mortal
I cannot look into your Heart and see your sorrow
Without it tearing me to pieces
Nor your rage
Nor even your Love
However; I certainly am capable of knowing myself in
those aspects
in order to heal or be a healer
in order to give another something other than my wounds
and receiving theirs once again
I must immerse myself in that which I am in the
emotional body

If I do what I have done so well
So many times and bury it
It will fester and grow beneath the surface
and untended and unloved
When it does erupt is more likely to be madness
more difficult to unravel, nearly impossible to understand
at the same time its impact will overthrow me

How can I not love you?
You show me your path
which is not an easy one
Awakening compassion for You
And a responding chord of compassion for myself
and others in the flesh

There is a faint glimmer in the back of my mind now
That shows these emotions in their Purity
Unsuppressed and fully accepted and integrated
and they are Beautiful and Vibrant with Life and Energy

As are you, my Prince
As are you.

Child of Love
01-01-13

I was born of Love
It is what I serve
It is what sustains me and keeps my feet on the ground
There is no other reason for me to be on the planet
and were it not for the demands of Love
Perhaps I no longer would be

When I rise its song is upon my lips
Whatever my actions in the day it is my counselor and guide
When I sit to listen to the stillness
It rises from within and sits by my side
It calls me from above and below
and supports my body when it aches

It is that which makes me rise and dance
It sings to me in every song that makes me aware
of my heart beating
the breath in my lungs
the cellular and molecular structure of that which
houses my Being
It aligns me
It shapes me
it is my one safe harbor
it is what called me to my Lover
and what carried us over many rocky shores
until our connection was forged in the fire of Love
and our songs blend in the dreamtime
whether we are awake or asleep

It is that which keeps me aware and caring of my tribe
Whether I have seen them seldom or often
when we meet again all is as it should be
the compersion never goes away
the remembering
the touching of hearts and minds and spirits
Revolve and renew within Love
Our differences fade into the background
as it is the one current that owns us all.

Free Falling
08-08-12

Given timely warning by runes and oracle
the day before
When I awoke and it felt like I was free falling
Through what I used to identify as self
and how I used to live my life
Two steps were taken
One acknowledging that I was not crazy and
understanding that change most desired can at moments
be the most difficult
Two letting go and asking for help
Which when I need it the most can sometimes be the
hardest time to ask
Surely this human experience is equally strange and wonderful

After receiving a steady stream of support all the way to work
I found myself laughing as my day in the world began
Though I still do not know why
But I do know that it is a trademark of the God I love
and She who is me but lives in the silence and the
timeless realm
Periodically in the last few weeks I have had delicious periods
Where She drives my consciousness and I get to witness
Far from being schizophrenic it is a complete union
Which is the sweetest most revelatory state of mind or being
I have ever known
The crossroads where meditation-poetry-communication
with Self and Gods
occurs
She has always been active in those periods; the One in
the driver's seat

So I am learning to be silent
not just in the short potent periods where I devote time
to meditation
But in my relations with others, there is a private space
where my introvert can live
Even within the active times when Spirit comes disguised
as what I formerly called
Mundane life

Today and the days going forward where I am free falling
and old parts of me tumble free from self-identity
I will approach it as a child climbing the ladder to the abandon
of slipping down the playground slide
With joy and laughter and a release of care
To that which provides it always
Whether I am aware in the moment or not

Instructions for the Care and Feeding of a Mortal
08-21-12

First of all, know your breed
Not everyone that looks like a Maenad is a Maenad
One may be marked with the taste for ecstasy
Have passion and love as well
But like an ex-showgirl
Those are simply marks of a past she has survived
I, for example, would have been dead on the streets
In my youth were it not for the protective force looking
after me
Which we will call Hermes

Secondly, you can break them
If you want a willing partner in the Great Work
You have to understand that they have limitations
Their circuitry is more fragile than yours
and if you are used to working with the advanced models
You may have to be patient with the beginner ones
If broken, the odds are that you will not be able to reassemble
To the same specs as the original
Or the rebuilt will not work as well

Thirdly, try a little tenderness
You may think that it is good to test and retest
To bring out their strength
To see their boundaries
To test their wisdom
Though these methods may work with some
Others will close up and look
For a more tender and responsive Deity
See above regarding breaking

Fourth and last,
Not every model that you find will be designed for you
These matches were made a long time ago
and though there is improvement over time
and they are evolving creatures
You will generally have those you can work with full time
as they were designed specifically for you
And those who happily will work with you part of the time
Under the guidance of their keeper

Please be aware that there is one unique Dorothea
She multi-tasks and is multi-faceted like no other
Do not expect any other human to come up to those standards
Or you will end up with too many broken ones
For the supplier to keep sending you more.

Portal of the Moon approaching Full Lunar Eclipse
11-27-12

The energies were such
expressing magic through the car radio
to carry me mostly uncomplaining through a two hour commute
with much crawling down Ashby Ave
in the city of Berkeley
while my spirit shook and shimmied and the car bounced
with my dancing
seat shaking
hands keeping time
While the music did its best to play me

Every brief glance of the nearly full moon in a sky black
and clouds scurrying across its face
Increasing the depth of the shifts in energy
Flowing flowing through and around me
with promises that the wild woman
Who has been peeking her head out the last two days
Will have her balance in the juggling of freedom and love
The taste of adventure on my tongue
Remembering the intensity of last night's long distance loving

My imagination soaring creating images of a thousand possibilities
Roads not yet explored
the deeper I go the further the expansion
as I lay down any agenda or even any desire other than
this fire
this combustion
pushing me out of the womb of Becoming
and dropping me into Being

Seeds that were planted this year
blow me kisses and tell me take your time
Let it unfold
this design that you create is a mirror image of
the Universe shaping you
The Master artist
Laughing as you stumble like a drunken child
and your carefree heart says oh baby
I am free at last
All is song and rhythm and movement
the gates are opening

When it gets bumpy approach it like a roller coaster
a wave to body surf
a dance step to learn while its movement is fresh
no fear here, take that first step, the sea below the
cliff entreats you

Shake and Bake
09-10-12

You live in my bones
I hear you rattling them at night
Shaking them as you make the divination
for the next God day in my life
Do You know that is probably a lifetime for me?

You live in my blood
Making it course hot and cold
Like the flow of some ancient river
Through beds of flesh
You drink me through Your desire
To absorb my sorrows and delight in my joys
Both determined by one quick toss of the dice
Both my lot in life
As long as mortal flesh holds me

You live in my tears
Salted, either warm through their fermentation in Love
or cold draining the selfishness from my being
Like a large cat I feel you lick them from my body
Just to make me giggle and laugh
Showing me the transitory nature of all I perceive

You live in my organs in all of my flesh
Your design is perfection
All works in harmony
When you have tuned me as one of your special tuning forks
To vibrate the note you want the Universe to sing
my organs and my sex reverberate as the rhythm
of your desire to Be
in all
drums through my mind

You create and procreate and recreate
I laugh when you give me the glimpse of how we
Co-create
Sometimes the wizard draws back the curtain
Except You are not diminished when I catch a glimpse of You
But all that is exists within Your being
and yet you can be as small as me
and vibrate through me without breaking me
On the contrary
You carry me on the edge of your transformation
Delicately
as the fiercest wave from the deepest ocean
Will let the surfer ride and deliver him to safe shore
Without breaking him.

The Angel
10-15-12

The moon brought clarity
Joy and acceptance
Learning, learning I am learning
When to fly
When to root so deep as to be unmovable
When to withdraw
and when to come forth

The angel came with His wings of fire
His heart of passion
His eyes of mystery
His gift was healing and pleasure and love
wrapped in an energy that contained all of this and more
I knew Him and I knew Him not
We had met recently on a flight when the worlds were
tasting the bliss
Of all opposites uniting
and the death of duality for all

Though none were ready to live there permanently
All had a taste so real so true
That the imprint was made
The template burned into consciousness

They tell me that the secrets
Are necessary since not even I can determine
The line between madness and bliss which blurs
in the moments of transformation
What my love, have I brought back from my perilous journey?
What gifts what fruits of sorrow and pain
What fruits of wisdom rising from the ashes
as that Phoenix is wont to do

I would not trade the gift of this lifetime
For anything in the universe
Other than spontaneous and total enlightenment for all
There is nothing else that would equal its preciousness to me.

My angel sits across the room and winks at me
A divine rogue
I will dream of Him tonight
in dreams of roses white and red
and the trembling of my soul
He will leave me with whispers I will try and remember
When the dawn surprises me once again.

Apollo

Phoebus Apollo

Ain't Gonna Write Rules for How the Universe is to Love Me

Alternate Reality

The Current of Full Moon in Virgo, Sun in Pisces

Will You Speak to Me

Phoebus Apollo
08-18-12

God of the Sun
Support of all living beings
Healer
Your light shines throughout Nature
As sunlight pours through a pane of glass
Or golden honey is drizzled on the offering

Through your gifts of art and music
You provide release from emotions which
would bring harm were they without outlet
Poetry and the company of the Muses
Bring the purest joy to human life
Transcending our mortality and revealing Spirit

Apollo
Son of Leto and Zeus
Your warmth and love
Are as Sun pouring through the crown of my head
Your light and gentle heat fills the body
Bringing immeasurable joy and peace
Rays of Your healing
penetrate the mind
causing synapses to spark with new connection

You have blessed Your Sons and Daughters
With the gift of sight
Allowing us the opportunity to course correct
before we stumble
This blessing from ancient times
More necessary than ever
Though few may be wise enough to seek You out.

Words fail to express what a vision today conveyed
Clouds and a blue sky with multiple rays penetrating
Reaching from the heavens toward the earth
The sight of it taking my breath away

Ain't Gonna Write Rules for How the Universe is to Love Me
02-08-13

Sometimes the grace hits
When you just cannot take any more
The light slides through the cracks in the darkness
When it is time for the germination process to begin
That last step into the crossroads
Brings the question you have carried like a burden
Too heavy to carry
Right to the surface and in your face
In the kindest way possible

I am not in charge here
and yet I cannot abdicate responsibility for the little
corner of the world
Where I stand
The Universe is smart enough to know when it should
whisper clues
and when it is more generous to let me flop about like a fish
Out of water
I learn from myself learning from IT
and I don't have to understand the process
or control it (ha ha)
To have it work exactly in the absolute best way
designed just for me

My role in my own life is changing
As I told a friend tonight
What absolutely terrifies me is that I do not get to
hide anymore
I love standing on the sidelines
Watching the dance proceed
Like watching the dance of traffic when Hermes is fully
in the drivers seat
It is a thing of great beauty and grace and perfect timing
But I am being brought to my adulthood
as I remember how to be a child

That which I learn is only a great joy to me
If I am able to share it
and that is when the real clarity kicks in

There are going to be major changes in my life
This coming Spring
I am not going to please everybody
Though I am going to try and tread ever so softly
Like a gazelle trying not to attract the lion's attention
My heart is wide open
My ears are listening
They are playing my song
I cannot possibly turn away from the part designed by
Us for me to play
You will hopefully forgive me if in the newness of it
My awkwardness causes you any discomfort.

Alternate Reality
08-05-12

She said " I am afraid I have drawn you into my alternate reality"
As if I had not chosen this path a thousand times
To be of service
To utilize all of who I am through love
To expand to learn to grow
and to do it in the best company possible.

If I am not consciously working in tandem with Spirit
I feel empty, without purpose, unfulfilled
that is a ripe feeding ground for all my addictive tendencies
The energy of every prayer, every act of sending or
receiving Reiki
Every meditation however brief
every ritual every initiation
every LBR, INRI and Middle Pillar
the ordeal of the Hep C treatment
the years of loneliness without awareness of
companions on the journey
or no knowledge of self other than what I had been fed
at a young age

All of this has brought me to this moment
and my heart is bursting with Joy
even as my body and mind are weary from the past few days

I wake up in the morning alive
Vital and attentive
Because each day brings me new understanding
whether it be a small step
or the overwhelming days that take me in leaps and bounds
Running with the chariot, and have to be reviewed and
processed later

There is only one other human being who knows how I feel
Without her and my love for her as catalyst
Much of this expansion and growth would not be
occurring at this time
and it is true
I pray that it is not moving too fast for me to stay grounded
To integrate in moments of peace these gifts more
precious than diamonds
as well as those moments when in unknown territory
sometimes hostile
I hang by a thread
But that thread is woven of the indomitable Love that is
the Universe
It is held in the hands of Fates and Gods
In truth though I may not feel it I know that though
it may appear to be only a thread
It is rope as strong as the highway between Earth and Heaven
the freeway that is my spine with me in the middle
between this seat on the ground
and the realms of all possibility
who through my Higher Self
Reach out to me to give me a hand up, and a place of
peace lit by lightning flashes.

The Current of Full Moon in Virgo, Sun Pisces
02-24-13

If I look within
The magnitude of the waiting stillness
is overwhelming
I sink into it like a haven
For all of me
Child who needs comfort
And an ancient part which is so tired
This journey in form
Again and again
Sometimes seems so heavy

Spirit rises each day
Joy is its name and birthright
Freedom is its song
Love anoints it bathes it refreshes it
The vibrations of the Sun
Within
increase as the opposition of Sun and Moon in its
perfect balance
Approach

If I can let go and allow the barriers to fall
Transformation will press its suit
and I
Its long lost lover
Will cleave to it and merge
finding no part that is not of it
Overflowing
Flooded with its energy
as it draws from the Universal Deep
to feed all these pockets of thirst
Which have never before been slaked

Each moment unique
and new
We think things are the same
We think that we are on repeat
But there is no such thing
The combination of all that makes up this
Here
Now
is Precious
Perfect
and full of Promise
as Completion occurs and flows and ebbs again.

Will You Speak To Me?
08-25-12

The candles are lit
The invocations read
The day begins when these are done
Though I have prepared myself in bed with self healing
Nothing truly signals the awakening of a new cycle
Until my hands are washed and my prayers
For alignment with the Heavens and Gods finished

There is a sweet stillness then
One which I do not want to leave
The Silence beckons to me
Embraces me
Whispers it is both Father and Mother
and I never want to leave that state
Yet it also reminds me that it is girding me to live in the world
To do whatever work it illuminates for me
To walk the path that is mine only to walk

Simplicity spoke to me last night
How can I not appreciate that what I give
may be loving support for another
and as I have recognized when on the receiving end
There really is nothing more important than that
We each have our assignments
and there is no such thing as great or small in these
As each of us is designed according to our nature
and the agreements we have made
But we need the shared strength and power
of Love which flames to full glory
When we are united within its bright Spirit
There is no shame in knowing that together we are More

My body carried a lot of my pain yesterday
Whether from old wounds healing
Or processing some too deep to reach the surface
I do not know
Meditation and contact with Higher Self
Removed some
But my stamina was flagging when I turned in early
the Citrine warm against my belly
Burst into full golden healing light
and I fell into sleep from that vantage point

These days are like a rare vintage wine that none have tasted.

Loki

Loki

Alternate Universe

Desert Song

Unpacking

Loki
(Revised 03-19-13)

The human body is not designed to ride a current of pure fire
Pure electricity running through its circuits
Relax, you say, and it is true
If I cannot let go and let You flow through me
I will blow a gasket

Laughing now and laughing then
Because at the same time my body is going oh NO
He is too BIG for me
There is an exhilaration at the PURE LIFE FORCE
of You
My cells alight with fiery energy are dancing
Free from doubts I am gifted by the flow of it
Even this double entendre makes me laugh
This time with Joy

Afterward I really wanted to jump something
But decided to lie down instead
Thinking I would sleep
But You still coursed through my veins
Through my chakras
Even closing my eyes
All was swirling spirals
As if my DNA was doing some mad hatter's polka
I chose the aquamarine crystal with pyrite
For its calming effect

Not certain whether it was purely the crystal
or a visit from Hermes
but I did drift off
Only to wake consistently all night long as the candle lit
for You
Burned brightly on its dual wicks

Continuously awake
My awareness embracing the feeling of Your protection
Nurturing self with Reiki
I tossed and turned
Yet on some deep level was content

I came to full consciousness with the alarm
With my thoughts wrapped in You
and a bone deep knowledge
That all would be well
It was inevitable
and my Heart and Spirit and Body
Were still alight with Your Sacred Fire

I am immersed in Love for You, Loki
You have shown me several aspects
I have felt Your laugh in my throat
and I have had Your scream of Rage tear through me
I have known Your compassion and Your humor
There is something irresistible in the attitude of Your stride
as I see You smoking a cigarette
Strutting down the street as if You own the World
And who would question that You do?

I have known the Power of Your cleansing fire
I have known the lengths that you will go to in order to Protect
Those sworn to You, Those that You love
My heart bears the imprint of Your rescues
and as long as I live I will remember
and a candle will burn upon Your altar.

Alternate Universe
01-31-13

How many dimensions did the car and I its passenger
Pass through this night?
A taste of the deepness
The brush of angel wings
the remembrance of making love on the astral
as my bliss body and I got reacquainted
and He who was catalyst
held the key to my locked chamber

The experiment tonight was
could I take the being I was at the height
of initiation
and let that being stay in that state
and live in another world
with different duties
While serving in full capacity as I am wont to do here and now
How would it feel?

The Universe responded
Gone for a bit was the pain
the somewhat unpleasant responses to
the processes of Western medicine to heal
and I was both the self I know
and another
in another plane who was
another me
and we exchanged gifts
we exchanged energies
Each acknowledging that our lessons and lives
were of value to ourselves in all our aspects

I am a messenger
I am a servant
I am a Priestess serving only Love
I am a warrior who will hold a point
Fearlessly
To the point of necessary sacrifice
Yet my life is precious to me

I am a poet
I am the song more than the singer
I am a teller of stories
of the future
of possibility
of love and truth and heroes and angels and Gods and all
those who love Them
I am a pool of sacred water, I am a spark of sacred fire

Desert Song
03-06-13

There was a loneliness deep
from the deepest point within its song arose
Slowly to the surface
Gaining momentum as it came
Like a midnight train sending sparks from the rails
that whistle that always haunts
the song was stark in its beauty and its austerity
As there was no one singing and no one to hear it

In the cool quiet darkness
the spark became a flame
Slender but strong
True to the center
Alone
Burning without fuel
perhaps it was its own fuel
as it neither diminished nor strengthened
in its timeless combustion
feeding off itself
as Love devours all but is not sated
nor hungry
but just IS

I live for the moments
The moments that capture me from within
The warmth rises from the heart
Descends from above
Rises from below
Some are heat that makes me want to holler
Some are comfort as if blanketing my child self
some are Mystery translating itself into that which is
FELT
prior to thought prior to word

Every poem written is a prayer
Begging for translation
of that which cannot be conveyed or explained
Into a message that may reveal itself
through a current that words ride upon
like a bareback rider on a restless stallion

Just as Spirit is revealed through flesh
Through Nature
Through the smile you send across the miles.
Seen only by the waiting heart.

Unpacking
11-03-12

This is new
I sit in this empty room
Asking if You want to write
Asking if there is a message that wants to be written
I ask of the core group whose company I was blessed
to keep
From the silence I wait for one voice to come forth
I have no agenda
I have time
I wait

* * * * * * * * * * *

You view my chaos and fire in its destructive face
as some kind of punishment
as some kind of evil
Yet can you not acknowledge that transformation comes at a price
of old facades tumbling down
and can you not accept that my ways of Loving
are about sweeping things clean
just as a forest fire will burn down debris and obstructions
To the light and to the seedlings of a new forest

Truly, you must make friends with me
I am not Your enemy
It is my influence that aids you in releasing so much
old patterning
So much clogging in the arteries that carry your hot
fresh blood
your Spirit created in Freedom
Has allowed itself to be bound
You have not stood in your freedom
nor used your free will wisely
It is out of Love and Love alone that We have come to
shake your foundations
To rattle your cages
To Enliven, Enlighten, and kick your asses
Whatever is necessary to wake you up

Can you honestly look around you
Look at the false constructs that you have overlaid on
this Perfect World
Its potential shining like a diamond
Pure and blazing
and tell me that you will not welcome this assist I offer you?
My fire blazes without to remind you that it blazes within
Mine the life force that created worlds and all living beings
From the primeval Void Who is My Bride
Wake up Wake up Wake up My children
You stand on the edge of Magnificence!

Orishas

Ellegua's Visit
01-12-93

Feeling Your energy sit upon my crown
I can only ask if You have a message for me
Though You are not deeply known to me
On the occasions when I have felt You near
my response is deep appreciation and gratitude and respect
Now I prepare a space to listen and write if You will

*   *   *   *   *   *   *   *   *   *   *

Children seek to understand who their parents are
When really all they should be doing is learning their lessons
When these children known as human beings come to
their adulthood
We will then have different conversations

I am understanding and not opposed to curiosity
I only counsel you to not confuse your priorities
If I come to you then I have a message for you
Instructions or perhaps I only wish to touch your mind
To bless you or to expand your consciousness and your
heart and spirit
Your emphasis on the power and value of your teeny tiny mind
is incomprehensible to me

When you lived in the darkness
When you had to hunt and be predator to simply survive
and feed your children
You developed skills in the mind
When you are involved in the areas of study, law, commerce
You use your mind, but is it not a bridge to the intuitive
gifts that allow you
To jump to the arenas of wild free consciousness
To listen and learn
To walk that bridge between Higher Self and those who
express Divinity
From the perspective of Being consciously that for
longer than you can ever comprehend

I would counsel you to learn to crawl, to learn to walk
Slowly and carefully and steadily
Then tell me how it feels to run to fly and to converse
with the Gods

Signing off now
"Big Daddy"

Heart Like a Stone
02-19-13

If I ever thought the crossroads was comfortable
Then I am a fool
I sit here now with my heart pounding feeling like there
is a stone inside me
All day vacillating between poles
and I sit here now
Knowing
In truth
That I have no idea which way to go

This is so foreign to me
Usually there is a slide to what feels natural and easy
Though even tonight I question my motivations
What started out as service in love and the sweetest of beginnings
Now leaves me sitting in the ashes of the bonfire
Wondering if I took a wrong turn

I know a little
I do not have a clue as to who or what the Orishas are
Sure I can read the stories
and I have tasted their energies more than once
and all I really know is
They are a whole lot bigger than me
They impact me and the world in ways I do not even
begin to understand
They come in all sorts of flavors but the underlying current is
Natural Power
As if they spring from draw their being from and feed
The earth Herself

How ancient they feel and yet
if they walk down the street personified
They are in tune with the times they manifest in
Tonight I feel lost and awkward without grace
and I am embracing this feeling right now
because at least I am feeling something
Rather than being frozen and immobile and stuck

I know that it is easy to demonize that which you are
unfamiliar with
But to deny one's reactions can also be to cut off the
early warnings
If one is truly in a dangerous situation
I have ignored messages from within more than once
and though I have not drowned I have had to tread water
in exhaustion and despair as a result

I am knocking at the door of my own innermost heart
Realizing that lack of sleep has some impact
But at the same time knowing that I am being herded like a cat
With the same amount of fur bristling
What is it really that I fear
Doors close and doors open
In the end the only thing I have as my compass
Is my prime directive
To serve Love

One cannot always see clearly
If lost in a thick fog
What sense does one have to rely on?
One can catch the scent of wet
ones footsteps still snug to the earth below
one's ears can hear silence or movement
There is a fine tuning that occurs when that white
blankets visibility

I fear change
I fear lack of change
I fear giving offense
I fear being untrue to myself and Those who love me
I fear being visible even more than I fear being invisible
I am used to that and it is familiar and safe
My introvert my hermit self like a crab draws into stasis
I fear vulnerability in the face of that which is not just
unknown
But exotic (which draws me in)
and carries a deep flavor of danger (which makes the hair
raise on my head)
at the same time that part of me is enticed
I fear my own madness

and even more than that, the part of me that clings to
the idea of sanity
and calcifies

More than anything I want to wake up in the morning
and have the answer, the signpost, the direction
painted on my bedroom wall
in fiery neon colors
with doubt blown to smithereens.

Standing at the Crossroads
01-20-13

Come child lay down your fears
The lies that tell you that you are separate from life
Are what bring you to the fear of death and that leads
To fear of everything that brings change
Is your heart so dark your vision so weak
That you cannot open it
When we come knocking?

Why do you suppose that those who have lived as guardians
of the pathways between life and death from the day
that Earth sprang to life
Are bringers of harm?
Again we question your knowledge of the wisdom of boundaries
Come child
Let your body dance away all these fears of the mind
Then come back and write some more

If your Spirit cannot be fierce and bold
Then why have you sought us?
Or if you have not sought us
Why the fascination?
Do you not know that every aspect of Big Daddy
Is fearsome in its capacity to protect
Which you appreciate
But also firm in its demands of discipline, study, truth, and
Self reliance
Why would we want our children to be weak and blind?
Has it occurred to you that you approach us to identify
and know and live from
Your core strength
Have you not asked that your every action be done from that
Source of integrity?

You, child, do not have to walk any path which does not
call to you
We do understand that your Heart's desire to serve the Good
Overrides all else
and we find no ill in this
Just be clear on your own motivations when you think of us
Or call us
We will make no demands
But you take care and make no bargains

Yes you can be friend to us with respect and care and
attentive love
We will keep you posted.

Crossroads Guardians
02-22-13

I can call you as Legba
as Hecate
as Odin
but whether you offered self to self hanging from a tree
after sacrificing your eye
or you guard the intersection between Life and Death
Or you personify the dark mysteries
You draw me in
yet there are times when I want to run

Where you stand between the worlds
is where the electricity flashes as lightning
or the current runs up and down my spine
with my hair standing on end
It is where I feel most alive
and most silent as your witness
or your temporary conduit
But you allow only a small tendril of what you are run through me
Or I would burn to a crisp in a second
Somewhat like the overload on amphetamine
Many years ago
When in the uncomfortable experience of Limbo

We mortals are funny creatures
We are children, and adolescents and adults
We are animal, human and divine
We go from a moment of understanding a glimpse of the mystery
to dropping down levels to where we have no clue in another
Sometimes we see your hidden hand which steadies
and loves us with great tenderness
and sometimes we only see the one that wields the power

and we think
If he has such power
why doesn't he just fix everything
why do we bleed, and suffer, and die
often times without knowing even why this sweet short
life has been lived
and the vast vision of aeons and aeons all running concurrently
is not available to us with your ease

We are challenged to stand on our own
as your children
and yet there are times when we overcome the terror of it
and we mouth off
we question
we even make demands
BUT please know this
It is only because we are young and always learning
and because you made us this way
inquisitive, free-willed, spirited, and brash
and my Lord and Lady
is it not your spirit within us that is so
and truly is it not much of what you love about us?

I sure hope so because I guarantee
with all the power of the Love I carry for you
We will test the limits again and again
So that we may know you and ourselves

Vision of the Orishas
02-20-13

I see them arise around me
As if awakening from their slumber
They are each beautiful brown skinned
oiled and lit as if the sun shown from within
Each one carries his/her own beauty and strength
Each has his unique function and abilities
One winks at me
and I know not who he is
But in that instant I remember
These are my friends my lovers my guides and teachers
From lifetimes gone by
When our camouflage colors matched

They say take it easy on Baba
We are working it out with him and you are both in the midst
of the same lessons
lessons arising all over the planet to your kind
lessons that you lived last summer
remember the key is the integration and receptivity with
your Higher Self
What was done naturally under the powers of Love and War
You now must learn under daily life
Though remember when the pressure cooker builds its
steamy force
It is to induce your reliance, trust and knowledge of
that beautiful part of you

Do not expect too much or too little from yourself
If you need to curl up in a ball sometimes
or just stay in bed with your cat be gentle and allow
what is necessary to the moment
and use this time to build your stock of compassion
You will need to draw on it for self and others more and
more as days go on
Remember that what you say to Hermes is true
What you offer is yourself, always
It is the love and devotion and dedication of your energies
that feeds us

When you put that energy into the food, the cigar, the
shot of rum
all is alive and blessed and fruitful

We have glimpsed your journey
We promise not to share it with you unless there is an
emergency need
You my darling one will have such joy in your struggles
and your relief
in your loving and your learning
In your falling down and rising up
We would not ruin a moment of you finding yourself
As Sam said but in another way
You are writing your story by living it
moment by moment
Breath by breath

As far as what we require from you
You will know when we tap you on the head
or whisper loudly in your dreams
Even that is part of the surprise

I say:
Ashe!
Iba Ashe!

Goddess

We Who are the Hidden

Freestyle

Mabon

Rooted in the Stone

You Shake Me

How Do I KNow You

Any Trick in the Book

Rain and Wave and Drops in the Ocean

Child of Madness

Lightning Strikes and the HEart Opens like a Flower

I am a Child Born of Two Worlds

We Who Are the Hidden
01-07-14

You do not see us unless we choose to become visible
Yet we are everywhere you are living
We cling to the old ways the old lands and territories
In between
In between time and in between space
We watch and we are still
Unless the demands of Those we serve
Bring us forth and draw action out of us

We came for the Earth
Called from our home in the Stars
We came by invitation by desire and by need
We came because we are called by service in tandem
With adventure
We did not know that for a time we would forget who
we were
But Remembrance lays across our shoulders
Like a mantle of lace or fur
Light and warm and natural
No fear no dismay and sorrow only when it is needed
As the great awakener

Watch for us
We are of your tribe and not of it
We have bred with the children of men
in order that you have the choice to survive
You are only required to find two things within
yourselves
Find courage and find love
Find the one and the other will rise from it naturally

We will be watching for you with joy in our eyes

Freestyle
09-22-12

I never rhyme
so here we go
I am just going to go with the flow

In the center of the circle
stands a woman clothed in purple
water flows at a gesture
air and fire have been sequestered
earth beneath her always stable
She has been here too long to remember
Who all her Allies are

Pure of heart her spirit free
All are drawn to her if Love they seek
Love it grows so exponentially
without effort like those southern vines that take over everything
a grid of light covers earth so easily
as all She is radiates freely
A gesture a smile and all is fulfilled
Those called to Her will be the Her children
when all is reborn

Mabon
09-22-12

Silent in the moonlit glade
All is sleeping except those who come to witness
the magic she weaves
as timeless as the earth and moon and stars
though they have changed their places in the sky
the constellations still remember
Her presence at the beginning of time

He laughs as He approaches
She has known Him in form and out
All that He is calls to Her
just as He is irresistibly drawn to Her
Two halves of a Wholeness
those without Love never understand
Their Union so powerful you feel the tremble in the land

They call to the elements to give their command
As change must now come
It is part of the plan
Whispered through the ages
By Priestess born women and men
The time now draws near
for them to make their stand
and though they are weary
Fire flows in their veins
True to their purpose
Only their Will remains

This night will end and morning approach
as the wheel it is turned
by Hearts true as theirs
All over the planet the work it is done
You think them alone
But they are a million to one
The tide it is rising You missed it when it began
Because it has been carried in the children of men
One may mean nothing a dozen nothing much more
But the millions whose light was hidden
Are rising this night

The dawn will be new and no stopping the Sun
The work finished then is already done
If you could read the records
You would flee when you can
this wyrd it is written by all of the Gods
and a multitude as great as the sands.

Rooted in the Stone
09-22-12

My flesh neither young nor old
My spirit both ancient and fresh and new
My heart timeless and the treasure house for Love
My mind an instrument that my Lady uses to tell me
secrets only she knows

Seasons change
transition from static to fluid
Winter and summer more fixed
Spring and Autumn more flexible
bringers of great change

Each time its own demands
Bringing forth its own gifts
When push comes to shove
You make the stand and You let the Largesse of the Universe
Deliver as it will

I can only demand of myself
All that I have to give
For those that I serve
Because I follow Their example
They have given me everything

They have given me Purpose
Forgiveness for my failings
Gentleness in the face of my fear
Love when I lay broken and still
Strength when I did not know how to carry on
and the remembrance of every moment where Love shone on me
Picked me up and carried me until I could heal
backup and regroup
Teachers and friends though sometimes few
Who were the very best shining examples of what
humans devoted to Spirit
and the Divine could Be
Bodhisattvas, and Buddhas, and Priestesses and Priests
and Shamans

So much to serve as example to inspire and to pull me forward
or on occasion in my youth give me a good swift kick
back into alignment

So Yes.
I will give my all
I will give until I can give no more
Then I will ask for You to strengthen me
so I can give more

Knowing that when I have done all within my capability
You will allow me time to rest and heal.

You Shake Me
09-22-12

You shake me up
You shake up the World Tree
You shake up my memory
You shake loose all the bits that no longer serve
You shake free the diamonds and the dirt
the love and the hurt
the freedom and the pain
and make all well again

You are both Young and Old
I know You as the most Ancient One
You carry the Soul of a World
as if it were a child's toy
at the same time that your Purity is Innocent and untouched
at the same time that Your passion burns so bright
That I must shield my sight

Everywhere I look I see Your face
In the vista of sky and clouds and sun
In the horizon
Which holds hills round and clothed in green
in the water stirred not shaken
with white caps dancing on it
as it mesmerizes me
In the faces of those that I see every day
and used to mistake for something other than your
representation in the world
Which all Life is

You sing within me
Like a new song and one that has haunted me forever
A melody that draws me home
Words that take me deeper and make the levels shift
around me
As You plumb all height and all depth with your message
Come home to Me
Come home to love
Come Home to Joy
Leave your fear and sorrow behind.

You have carried life as a burden far too long
when truly it is a Gift
The Gift of Me within all that is.

How Do I Know You
01-08-14

I introduce myself to Her
As I seem to know/not know Her
It feels right to offer my morning walks at work
To Her
Especially the struggle up the hill

Today there were so many birds around
It felt as if they were sending greetings
and She understood
To me it was a beautiful communication though
My ears heard only part of the song

I asked Her to tell me who She was
Of the Gods I know I have learned that They have gone so FAR
Beyond their origin stories, or the myths we read
I did not want to just research Her stories

There was a brief flash
If She knows me She knows that I am not by nature
Strong visually
and that form of discourse always thrills me
and makes me sit up and pay attention

The flash was of a strong and beautiful female
in the forge
muscles gleaming
as the sweat rolled off her body
There was the sight of red hot metal
Thrust into the water to cool
Steam rising

She speaks:

Child you have tasted Me in healing
and I have passed through you in inspiration
As your fingers did their very best to dance across the keyboard
But I ask of you especially
To look to the physical

To look towards the needs of the body
Look to what brings fire and vitality
Move
Work physically
Dance
Take care of your sustenance
Both energetically and in food and drink
Nourish yourself that you may nourish others

We touched on it last night
That it was never Me that you fear
But yourself
You have hidden yourself for a very long time
and you feel safe in the deep waters
invisible
But you are no Nyad
nor Undine
You have sworn yourself and you have begged to be of service
I tell you that you must learn to hold your boundaries
and be visible

You have seen the connections dance in the air
Under all environments
In large gatherings where you wanted to hide
At work where you like to pretend it is all alien
I tell you that you make it hard by denying your place here
You look to your sisters and see strong resilient and beautiful women
You will never know the courage that they have earned step by step
Nor will you know your own if you cannot take your own steps
and know which boundaries are your sacred own
and which you are meant to cross in sacrifice for the whole

I know your thrill when you saw me shaping iron
This image holds a lot
Think of the iron when you ground
Think of the fire and water that shape it into a fierce tool
and get to work.

Any Trick In the Book
01-13-14

It's always about the love
The Shaper works in the forge
or at the hearth
with pen in hand
or within the thousand ways of healing

The Universe in its infinite Love and Creativity
Hones itself into special aspects
To entrap our curiosity
or to simply make the adventure of Truth and Love
So irresistible that nothing else holds a candle to it

This Goddess
This Being
has so many tricks up Her sleeve
How can I do anything but adore Her?

She can capture my mind
My emotions
The sweat off my skin in karma yoga
awaken my compassion and teach skillful means
How can I be anything but deeply in love with Her?

Endlessly calling us in
the lure always before us
The allure
This whole Universe designed upon the absolute power and draw
of Love in action

We may fall down, fall apart, fall to pieces, fall behind
But the underscore
the basis
the field, the open plain where all exists
Rests in this ground of being which is always and only
The interplay of Love in Creation

Oh Brigid, you model it so very very well.

Rain and Waves and Drops in the Ocean
01-15-14

She tells me that she is small and unimportant
Right before I give her an opportunity
To be of some use in the moment
Reminding her that the cycle of rain and drought
or rivers struggling to clear themselves
or the earth weeping as it cannot free the waters from
the poisons
of men

are tools to teach
as well as a call and response.

When it rains hard
the earth will receive and then the torrents will move
They will move obstructions
They will move to break down damns
or to fill the beavers pond
They will tumble as waterfalls
or cleanse that which has become stale or brittle or simply stuck
in patterns that are no longer alive and kicking

Remember that what you form as images in your minds
With fierce intent
can aid the waters of the world
You have within the memories of pure still pools
of the lakes and beaches of your childhoods
clean and clear and deep and healing
The streams that you may have fished in
With no care as to whether you caught one or not
but just the joy of baby trout nibbling on your toes
Daughters of Earth and Water
Air and Fire

You hold the templates within yourselves
To Heal and recreate the world around you
Take action where you can on every level
But always remember you carry the Sacred Waters
within your very beings
Allow them to come forth as if your very lives depend on such
Transformation.

Child of Madness
1-16-14

You who look at me with questions in your eyes
I cannot help that you do not know me
My heart
My spirit
My enslavement willingly to Love
I have had my course set for me
as an answer to all of my prayers
I cannot live for anyone other than
Those I am promised to

If I do not speak the words running through my mind
As they are gifted to me
Then is the only time that my Spirit is crushed
So I choose with all that I am this late in the game
To be who and what I am
If I stumble or fail it is only for the Gods and I
myself to determine
This voice that tells me that I am whole
and must only know it and be it
Is terrifying and healing at the same time

I adore my kith and kin
My allies
But I know that it is an irrational fear
that drives me to hide myself from them
Yet expose myself to the world
I surrender to the Perfection of Love
in community
If I am not accepted as I am
Then it does me no avail
to deny it

She whispers in my ear
«You remember the joy of vulnerability whilst being
naked in your presentation
I will tell you when and if you need to be invisible
I will be your shelter then»

Lightning Strikes and the Heart Opens Like a Flower
02-05-14

Thrown out of meditation by the sheer rush
of the knowledge that I am completely deeply and irrevocably
In passionate love with Universe
as manifest in Deity
in Dragons
in cats
in rain storms
in sunshine
in Trees
Oh My God trees

It struck me blowing the heart wide open
I had connected the core beneath the navel
with the anvil at my feet
feet had been growing roots
I followed the trunk that I imagine to be my backbone
to the magnificent oak over my head
the energy of stars and moon came coursing down
through the crown
and heaven and earth energies merged in the heart

Then I had one thought
I love Hermes
followed by I love Brigid
Then Loki
Then the energy just ramped up and I realized I LOVED
EVERYTHING
That this temple I live in
With these symbols of Gods and Goddesses and Divine Beings
Chinese Dragons with pearls of wisdom
Is teeming with Pure Chi

Nothing is symbolic
This room vibrates with These Energies
My bedroom houses aspects of These Gods
The crystals that I use in healing
Share their life force as freely
as the cat from the streets
who tenderly lays his head on my chest

There is only Love
It is Life
It is Source for all that is Manifest
It is Source for all that is Hidden
and I a mere child
Sit enthralled by the merest touch of its energy going
ping in my heart

The healer who worked on me tonight is Doctor Maia

I am a Child Born of Two Worlds
03-19-14

I am a Child of the Gods
Born by choice in a time of need
Child of Earth
Child of Stars and Sea
Child old before my time
Child reborn in the Burning Heart
Child of Water
and Child of Stone
Recognizing more and more
I am my Mother's daughter

Child with feet that dance
a voice that sings
Embracing the seasons
year by year
The wheel turns
like a mill wheel it grinds
and brings our return.

The bindings are falling
my limbs and heart free
I feel more and more all the others like me
The chains they are tightening
Love is their forge
False memories departing
Torn away by the storm

My guardians thrill me
Even if pain evens the score
No price is too high for the end of this war
Within and without
Again and again
I surrender in peace
Love is the answer
Still all that I need.

About Concrescent Letters

Concrescent Letters is dedicated to publishing unique works of Poetry and Prose. It takes advantage of the recent revolution in publishing technology and economics to bring forth works that, previously, might only have been circulated privately.

Now, we are growing the future together.

Colophon

This book is made of Mistral and Dakota, using Adobe InDesign. The cover was designed, the body was set by Sam Webster. Cover photo was taken by the author.

Visit our website at
www.Concrescent.net

www.ingramcontent.com/pod-product-compliance
Lightning Source LLC
Chambersburg PA
CBHW030524100426
42813CB00001B/145